SHOCK ZONE™
TRUE SURVIVAL STORIES

SuRVIVING
ANIMAL
ATTACKS

BY PATRICIA NEWMAN

Lerner Publications Company • Minneapolis

Cover photo: A grizzly bear shows its teeth.

Lerner Publications Company
A division of Lerner Publishing Group, Inc.
241 First Avenue North
Minneapolis, MN 55401 U.S.A.

For reading levels and more information, look up this title
at www.lernerbooks.com.

Library of Congress Cataloging-in-Publication Data

Newman, Patricia, 1958–
    Surviving animal attacks / by Patricia Newman.
        pages   cm — (Shockzone. True survival stories)
    Includes index.
    ISBN 978-1-4677-1435-8 (lib. bdg. : alk. paper)
    ISBN 978-1-4677-2511-8 (eBook)
    1. Animal attacks—Anecdotes. 2. Animal behavior—Anecdotes. I. Title.
QL100.5.N49 2014
    591.5'3—dc23   2013022636

Manufactured in the United States of America
1 – PC – 12/31/13

TABLE OF CONTENTS

Imagine losing your arm to an alligator or your face to a chimpanzee. Imagine being slashed by a grizzly bear or nearly **bitten in two by a shark.** These aren't just frightening imaginary scenarios. These things have actually happened to adults and children who survived brutal animal attacks.

When people enter an animal's territory, there's no telling when an attack might happen.

Animals have many amazing ways to defend themselves and get food. Some sting. Others bite or claw. Animals may attack out of fear or hunger or because they feel threatened. Maybe a child pulled a dog's ears. Perhaps a swimmer reminded a hungry shark of a tasty seal. A mother bear might have thought a hiker threatened her cubs. Whatever the reason, someone who triggers an animal attack could face extreme danger. Read on for true stories from people who lived through this danger. The victims all showed courage and fought hard for survival.

A Grisly Grizzly Attack

"Oh no!" Jenna cried. Terrified, she backed up. Just then, her dad spotted the grizzly bear in their path. Razor-sharp teeth. Ears flattened in anger. There was no time to run, hide, or even think. In two leaps, the bear attacked.

Jenna and Johan Otter were celebrating Jenna's graduation from high school. They were on a father-daughter trip to Glacier National Park in Montana in 2005. Just before nine o'clock on a warm August morning, they were deciding how much farther to walk. They were both in excellent physical shape. Johan ran marathons and Jenna danced.

The trail followed a ridge on a cliff. Jenna took the lead. She climbed rough steps cut into the trail. She stopped to admire the beautiful view. A golden eagle flew above them in blue skies with high clouds. It skimmed the tops of tall pine trees. Johan paused to snap pictures.

Farther up the trail, a boulder blocked their path. Jenna scooted around it. Behind the boulder was a mother grizzly bear with her two cubs. Jenna's sudden appearance startled the grizzly. Grizzlies don't attack people often. But when they feel their cubs are threatened, they won't hesitate to defend their territory. When Johan saw the grizzly, he jumped in front of Jenna to protect her. The animal leaped and bit into his left thigh. The red can of pepper spray intended to stop animal attacks flew out of the mesh pocket of his backpack.

"I didn't fight back," Johan later said. "I couldn't. The bear was throwing me around." Johan worried that the grizzly would tear him apart. "I looked down the trail and decided the best thing to do was to get myself off the slope." Johan ripped his body out of the bear's jaws and rolled off the ledge. He tumbled down a steep hill over rocks and brush. Meanwhile, up on the ledge Jenna scrambled for the can of pepper spray. The bear growled. Jenna fumbled with the safety cap.

Mother grizzlies are fiercely protective of their cubs.

Even after Johan and Jenna fell down a slope, the grizzly continued chasing and attacking them.

When he reached the bottom of the slope, Johan looked back up. He realized the bear was still on the ledge with his daughter. "Come down here!" he yelled to Jenna. "It's safe!"

The bear reared up, towering over Jenna. She fainted from terror and tumbled off the ledge 50 feet (15 meters) to the rocks below. When she hit the rocks, she broke her back.

"It's unbelievable how fast grizzlies barrel up and down slopes," Johan remembered. He curled in a tight ball to protect himself as the bear rushed toward him. It grabbed him by his pack and shook him like a doll. Johan managed to rip himself away from the bear again. He fell another 30 feet (9 m) down the slope. The bear followed. It gnawed Johan's head, scratched with its claws, and bit his right arm. After Jenna's fall, she had crawled behind a rock under low-hanging branches. Her father's screams pierced the air. When the screaming stopped, she did not know if he was alive or dead.

Johan rolled away from the bear one last time. He fell onto rocks at the edge of a steep cliff. Above was the ferocious grizzly. Below was a drop of several hundred feet. The bear followed him to the cliff's edge, but this time, Johan played dead. The bear nosed around for a while before moving away. Then Jenna screamed. "That was the worst sound I've ever heard," her father said.

A fully grown grizzly bear can weigh nearly 800 pounds (360 kilograms).

Heavy panting told Jenna the grizzly had returned for her. Her heart raced. She held her breath and remained still as the bear's nose poked through the branches. She hit it with her fist, and it bit her head. Jenna played dead. Eventually the bear lumbered away.

After Johan was sure the bear had moved on, he called to Jenna. He felt incredible relief when he heard his daughter's voice. They yelled for help for forty-five minutes before a group of hikers found them. Two hours later, the park's medical staff arrived. Four hours after that, a helicopter hovered over the trail to lift them out.

Expert medical care saved Johan's life. The bear had cracked the bone around his right eye. One bite snapped his wrist. Other bites broke his nose and spine. In all, twenty-one bite and claw marks covered his body. He required several surgeries. Jenna's broken back kept her from dancing for several months. But by spring, she began practicing in the studio again.

The Otters' evacuation by a rescue helicopter saved their lives.

NO SMOKING WITHIN 50' of HELI PAD or ANYWHERE on KRMC CAMPUS

STOP
IF HELICOPTER IS RUNNING, THIS AREA IS EXTREMELY DANGEROUS!
DO NOT PROCEED UNTIL HELICOPTER SHUTS DOWN OR TAKES OFF
THANK YOU! ALERT

Johan returned to the Glacier National Park trail only eleven months after the attack. Jenna waited three years before returning. Finishing the trail helped Johan and Jenna tame the grizzly that haunted their dreams. They learned to enjoy nature again. "Grizzlies are a sign of true America," Johan said. "They are a symbol of wilderness at its purest—and of an ecosystem that is intact. You need to be really respectful of that and the dangers that go with it."

ecosystem = a group of living things that interact to survive

BEAR COUNTRY CLUES

Watch out for the following clues when you are hiking in bear country. If you see one or more of these, be on the lookout for bears in the area.

- Do you see overturned rocks? A bear may have been looking for food.
- Are there birds circling in the sky? They might be waiting for a bear to finish eating a dead animal.
- Are there rushing streams nearby? These are perfect bear fishing spots. The water makes it harder for bears to hear hikers.
- Is the wind blowing in your face? The bear won't smell you coming, meaning you are more likely to surprise it.

When you're walking through the woods, make noise, talk, or tie bells to your hiking stick. If a bear hears you coming, it is more likely to avoid you.

Johan had to wear a special device to keep his neck still during the healing process.

THE SCORPION QUEEN

Staff Sergeant Monique Munro-Harris of the US Air Force was sound asleep at Kirkuk Regional Air Base in Iraq in November 2006. Suddenly she felt something crawling on her ear. "I swiped at [it] with my left hand," she said. "Whatever was on there stung my ring finger. It hurt, but I guess I was still groggy because I really didn't react to it."

When she felt another sting near her left armpit, she jumped out of bed. She shook her blankets and danced around. "This time it had my full attention," she said. "I knew there was something in my room that shouldn't be there, and I wasn't going back to bed until I found it."

A yellow scorpion lay at her feet. It was dead. She had accidentally stepped on it when hopping around. The scorpion's tail was thin. Its pincers were tiny. It measured about 5 inches (13 centimeters) in length. Munro-Harris had arrived at the base three months before. Her job was to repair medical equipment in support of the war in Iraq. She knew she might have to dodge explosions and bullets. But scorpions were not on her radar.

Munro-Harris scooped the scorpion into an empty Q-tip box. She felt fine. "Not even a bit sick," she remembered. Still, just to be safe, she walked to the base hospital. Within a few hours, Munro-Harris started shaking. "My breathing was feeling funny... my throat felt like it was starting to close," she said.

Most scorpion stings are no more harmful than bee stings. But the public health officer on base identified Munro-Harris's scorpion as a deathstalker. It is one of the deadliest scorpions in the world. The poison travels through the victim's body very fast. The victim soon develops a fever. Heart rate and blood pressure skyrocket. Fluid fills the lungs. The victim usually dies from heart failure.

Deathstalkers live throughout the Middle East and North Africa.

"We didn't have antivenin at our facility," remembered Major Amy Gammill, the doctor on duty at the base hospital. Within minutes, Munro-Harris passed out. The only antivenin available was at another base. Doctors prepared Munro-Harris for a forty-five-minute helicopter ride to Joint Base Balad.

antivenin = medicine to heal someone who has been bitten by a venomous animal

"Simply flying to Balad is very risky," said Colonel Patrick Storms, Kirkuk's flight surgeon. "The reality is that you can be shot down." For Munro-Harris, getting shot down was the least of her worries. Halfway through the flight, her blood pressure fell to zero. "You can do that for about four minutes before you die," Storms said. Reduced blood flow to the brain can lead to brain damage.

Storms pumped Munro-Harris full of a drug to jolt her heart into pumping enough blood to save her organs. He brought four syringes along for the trip and emptied all four. When they arrived at Balad, doctors injected the antivenin into Munro-Harris. After about eleven hours, she was flown to Landstuhl Regional Medical Center in Germany.

Munro-Harris was flown to Joint Base Balad on a UH-60 Black Hawk helicopter.

To create antivenin against the venom of scorpions, snakes, and other animals, scientists must first collect a venom sample.

"I woke up confused," Munro-Harris said. "I didn't know what happened, where I was or how close to death I'd come. And I was in pain. It felt as though someone had been standing on my chest." Thanks to the quick action of doctors, Munro-Harris recovered completely and returned to duty at Kirkuk. "I'm just grateful the military has such awesome doctors. I definitely wouldn't be here today without them."

SCORPION TOXIN FIGHTS CANCER

One of the ingredients of deathstalker venom may actually be used to help heal people instead of harming them. Brain surgeons have a difficult time separating brain tumors from healthy brain cells. Cut too little and the cancer remains. Cut too much and the patient suffers. But what if there was a way to highlight the cancer cells before operating? One deathstalker venom ingredient attaches to brain cancer cells and lights them up, making it easier for surgeons to see which cells to remove.

Pet Dog Attack

Seven-year-old Canadian Tyler LeClaire arrived at his older sister's home after hockey practice in January 2013. He planned to log some serious gaming time while his dad ran errands. LeClaire plopped in front of the TV next to a dog belonging to his sister's boyfriend. The dog had snapped at LeClaire in the past—still, the boy never expected what happened next. The dog suddenly lunged at him. It bit him in the face, pulling off the boy's cheek.

The family sprung into action right away to get LeClaire the help he needed. They called 911. Paramedics rushed LeClaire— and the skin the dog had bitten off—to the hospital so that doctors could reattach the skin. LeClaire was taken into surgery, where doctors successfully repaired his cheek.

While he was in the hospital, two members of LeClaire's favorite professional hockey team visited him. They gave him a signed Calgary Flames jersey. "It was a nice visit," LeClaire's dad said. "It was the first time I saw Tyler smile in a while." Sixteen days after the surgery, doctors removed LeClaire's stitches. They said he'd have only a small scar once his wound had completely healed.

No one knows why the dog attacked LeClaire. Although the dog had snapped at him before, she had also played with him only days before the attack, showing no signs of aggression then. After the attack, the dog had to be euthanized to prevent any future attacks. The owner was also fined $450.

euthanized = killed painlessly. Sick or dangerous animals sometimes have to be euthanized.

Two months after the attack, LeClaire ended up having to have a follow-up surgery. Doctors weren't satisfied with the way the cheek was healing. They say he may need additional operations too. Yet LeClaire and his family are very thankful that his cheek was repaired and that his injuries weren't more serious than they were.

ANIMAL CONTROL 761

When pets attack, animal-control workers often take the animals away.

Torn Apart by a Chimpanzee

"He's killing my friend!" Connecticut woman Sandra Herold screamed at the 911 operator. "Send the police out with a gun! Hurry please!" Earlier that evening, Herold called her friend Charla Nash to help get Herold's pet chimpanzee, Travis, back into her house. When Nash stepped out of her car, the 200-pound (91 kg) chimp attacked.

Chimps are incredibly strong. Travis grunted and shrieked in anger. He bit apart Nash's hands. He broke most of the bones in her face. Nash screamed in pain. Travis ripped off a large portion of her scalp, along with her nose, lips, and eyelids. Herold stabbed Travis with a butcher knife. She then hit him over the head with a shovel. But nothing distracted Travis from his brutal twelve-minute attack on Nash. Finally, the police arrived. Travis approached their cars, knocking off a passenger-side mirror with a swing of his arm. He then walked around to the driver's side, opened the door, and attacked the officer inside. The officer quickly drew his weapon and shot Travis multiple times. The chimp ran off into the woods. Following a trail of blood, officers finally found him dead in his cage at home.

Travis was fourteen years old and had been an animal actor. He had performed in commercials for Old Navy and Coca-Cola. Herold treated him like a son. He ate steak and lobster at the dinner table. He drank wine from a glass, used the toilet, and bathed himself. Travis used a computer to look at photos and surfed TV channels. He even brushed his teeth and watered plants!

"It's hard to say what exactly precipitated this behavior," said Colleen McCann, an ape specialist at the Bronx Zoo in New York City. "[Chimps] are not human and you can't always predict their behavior and how they... will respond when they feel threatened."

precipitated = caused

Nash had survived the brutal attack. Now, her survival was in the hands of her surgeons.

Herold (*left*) and her husband went out in public with Travis often.

At the hospital, doctors created a hole in Nash's face to give her lifesaving fluids. They removed her damaged eyes. Nash wore a hat and veil for almost two years to hide her face. "I wear it so I don't scare people," she said. She also wanted to reveal her injuries on her own terms rather than allow a photographer to sell the images to the highest bidder. Nash's doctor said, "Charla didn't attend her daughter Brianna's high school graduation because she thought her presence would take away from the day."

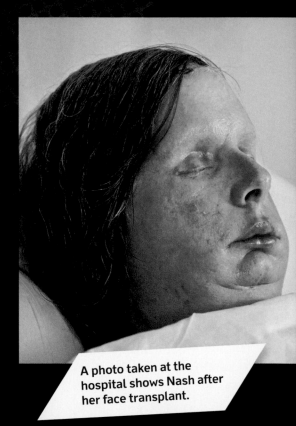

A photo taken at the hospital shows Nash after her face transplant.

Nash does not remember the vicious attack, but she recalls that Travis had always scared her. "One time he was running around the yard and swinging off the trees of the house, and he jumped on my back and he pulled a big hunk of hair out of my head. I had tears in my eyes and [Sandra] was laughing and I told her, 'It hurts.'"

A tragedy affecting another family made it possible for Nash to receive hand and face transplants. Her donor had died in an accident. A team of more than thirty doctors and nurses operated on Nash for twenty hours. "That donation, as hard as it was for them, was a wonderful gift for me and my family," Nash said. "It really gave me a life back."

For the first time in two years, Nash ate solid food. She also began breathing through her nose. Eventually, her new face should fit well on her bone structure. But soon after the surgery, Nash developed an infection that affected circulation to her new hands. Doctors had to remove them. She looks forward to another hand transplant and getting a guide dog. Nash also hopes to attend her daughter Brianna's college graduation.

WHY CHIMPS SHOULD NOT BE PETS

Some people buy baby chimpanzees as pets because they are cute. But when the adorable babies grow up, they are much stronger than adult men. An angry adult chimp can be deadly. If one gets upset, it can cause serious damage to people and property.

Nash (*right*), speaking with her lawyer (*left*), was given another shot at life, thanks to amazing medical technology.

BIG JOE STRIKES

One hot August day near Slidell, Louisiana, twelve-year-old Devin Funck and his friends went swimming in Crystal Lake. Without warning, a 500-pound (227 kg) alligator locked its jaws around Funck's wrist and elbow. The alligator dragged him to the bottom of the lake. Its claws sliced into Funck, and its jaws ripped his left arm off at the shoulder. His friends ran for help as he managed to escape the alligator and reach the shore. "I thought I still had my arm," he said, "and I looked and I was like, 'Oh, man!'" Sheriff's deputies rushed Funck to the hospital.

Earlier that day, Funck and his pals had spotted the alligator on a far bank. Residents of the area were familiar with the 11-foot (3.4 m) alligator known as Big Joe. When they first saw it, one of the boys threw sticks in its direction. Perhaps Big Joe thought a tasty turtle splashed nearby. Funck planned to keep an eye on the alligator when he went swimming. But Big Joe outsmarted him. The crafty reptile slipped underwater and swam straight for Funck.

Deputy Howard McCrea found and killed Big Joe later that day. Still standing in ankle-deep water, McCrea cut open Big Joe's belly to retrieve Funck's arm. Officials placed the arm in an ice chest and rushed it to the hospital. Unfortunately, too much time had passed for doctors to reattach Funck's arm. Funck would be an amputee.

amputee = a person whose arm or leg was lost in an accident or operation

At a community fund-raiser to help pay for his medical bills, Funck received Big Joe's stuffed head. "It takes my arm, I take its head," Funck said. Even after surviving a terrifying attack, he still kept his sense of humor.

About 1.5 million alligators live in Louisiana.

Attacked by a Shark, Saved by Dolphins

Bam! Something had just hit Todd Endris's surfboard hard and fast. He flew off his board. "Maybe I saw [it] a quarter second before it hit me." But that wasn't enough of a warning. The giant shark rushed by him and circled around for another attack. "It just shows you what a perfect predator they really are," Endris later said. Endris climbed back onto his surfboard. Belly on the board, he paddled toward shore as if his life depended on it—because it did.

Bam! Another hit, then heavy pressure engulfed Endris's back. The shark had sandwiched Endris and the surfboard in its jaws. "I reached behind me and punched at the shark's face...hard as I could." Rather than stopping, the shark's jaws only got tighter. "It was obvious I was no match for this machine of a fish."

Suddenly the shark let go. Endris was free. He floated in water stained red with his own blood. But the attack was far from over. The shark struck again. This time, it bit into Endris's right leg. He kicked it in the face and shouted, "Help! Somebody help me!"

Clicks and squeaks began filling the air. Sleek gray shapes slipped through the water around him. Then one burst through the surface. "Something leaped out of the water...over my head," Endris said. A group of dolphins had formed a protective circle around him.

Dolphins are known for playing with and protecting people in the water.

Another surfer several yards away shouted at Endris to get on his board. "With every ounce of strength I had left, I hoisted myself onto it," he remembered. The pair floated together toward the shore, still encircled by dolphins. "I don't remember much else after that," Endris said. A surfer on the beach also helped save his life. Blood pumped from Endris's leg at an alarming rate. The surfer used Endris's surfboard leash to make a tourniquet. Doctors said the shark nearly punctured one of Endris's lungs and bit his leg to the bone. "I lost half of my blood in the attack and spent six days in the hospital," Endris said. His injuries required five hundred stitches and two hundred staples.

tourniquet = something tied around a limb to stop bleeding

Endris's mother reminded him that he loved the ocean for its beauty. "Think about the good things," she told him. Endris followed her advice. He remembered how fog settled on Monterey Bay the morning of the attack. He recalled the touch of a tuna's fin as it brushed his leg. Most of all, he remembered the surfer who coached him to shore after the attack and the dolphins who saved him. "The sea held dangers, but it held angels, too," Endris said.

Six weeks after the attack, Endris was back at the water's edge, a surfboard under his arm. Endris began studying areas that sharks frequented so he could avoid them when he surfed. "Part of me wanted to run away, but I had to get back into the water. Once I was on top of my first wave, everything else faded away. I was alive!"

AVOID BECOMING A SHARK VICTIM

- Animals that splash are usually in trouble. This makes them targets for sharks.
- Shiny jewelry glistens like fish scales. Bright bathing suits look like pretty fish. Leave the bling at home.
- Smell is a shark's superpower. They can smell a few drops of blood from far away. Don't swim if you are bleeding.
- If you do get bitten, don't try to yank yourself out of the shark's mouth. It will eventually release you.
- Eyesight is critical for sharks. Hit its eyes, not its nose.

Endris refused to let his brush with death stop him from pursuing his love of surfing.

1. Hippopotamus: these beasts may look peaceful. However, they weigh up to 8,000 pounds (3,600 kg), run as fast as 20 miles (32 km) per hour, and can use their huge mouths to crush like a sledgehammer.

2. Australian box jellyfish: these creatures have sixty tentacles, each up to 15 feet (4.6 m) long. Their sting can kill a human.

3. Great white shark: these ferocious sharks are about 15 feet (4.6 m) long as adults. Their huge jaws hold three hundred jagged teeth.

4. Grizzly bear: grizzlies weigh up to 800 pounds (360 kg). When they stand on their back legs, they are 8 feet (2.4 m) tall. They can run 35 miles (56 km) per hour.

5. Cape buffalo: these buffalo are aggressive, unpredictable, and weigh up to 1,800 pounds (816 kg). They kill more than two hundred people per year.

6. Elephant: elephants are the heaviest land animal, weighing up to 15,000 pounds (6,800 kg). They can be unpredictable, and their legs can crush almost anything.

7. Crocodile: crocs can be up to 20 feet (6 m) long. Their ears, eyes, and nostrils are on the top of their heads so they can track prey while hiding underwater. They kill up to eight hundred people per year.

8. Lion: these mammals combine incredible speed with razor-sharp claws and teeth. They stalk prey silently, and then rush at their targets in bursts of speed up to 50 miles (80 km) per hour.

9. Snake: out of more than 3,000 snake species in the world, about 450 are venomous. More than half of these can kill a person. The carpet viper causes the most snakebite deaths worldwide.

10. Mosquito: these insects kill more than 1 million people per year worldwide. They do this by spreading diseases, such as malaria, West Nile virus, and yellow fever.

American Museum of Natural History. *Animal Life: Secrets of the Animal World Revealed.* New York: DK, 2011.
This book is great for animal lovers. It features many color photographs and fascinating facts.

Barr, Brady, and Kathleen Weidner Zoehfeld. *Crocodile Encounters and More True Stories of Adventures with Animals.* Washington, DC: National Geographic, 2012.
Check out these action-packed stories from a real-life crocodile scientist.

Claybourne, Anna. *100 Deadliest Things on the Planet.* New York: Scholastic, 2012.
Ferocious animals, deadly storms, and burning volcanoes are just some of the fascinating topics waiting for readers in this book.

Curry, Don. *The World's Deadliest Creatures.* New York: Discovery Channel, 2008.
This book gives readers a brief introduction to the characteristics, habitat, and habits of the world's deadliest creatures.

Doeden, Matt. *Deadly Venomous Animals.* Minneapolis: Lerner Publications Company, 2013.
For some animals, all it takes to kill is a single bite or sting. Check out this book to learn more about all kinds of deadly venomous animals.

Higgins, Nadia. *Deadly Adorable Animals.* Minneapolis: Lerner Publications Company, 2013.
Just because an animal looks all cute and fluffy doesn't mean it won't bite! Read this cool book to find out which friendly-looking animals are actually dangerous.

LERNER

SOURCE

Expand learning beyond the printed book. Download free, complementary educational resources for this book from our website, www.lerneresource.com.

7   Julie Cederborg, "Survival Story: Surviving a Grizzly Attack in Glacier National Park," *Backpacker*, October 2006, http://www.backpacker.com/survival_guide_skills_survival_story_surviving_grizzly_attack_glacier_national_park/skills/12227.

8   Ibid.

9   Ibid.

11 Ibid.

12 Tim Barela, "The Scorpion Queen—Airman Barely Survives Sting from One of the World's Most Venomous Creatures," *US Air Force*, January 1, 2010, http://www.torch.aetc.af.mil/news/story.asp?id=123196043.

13 Ibid.

13 *WFMZ-TV 69 News*, "Local Woman on Animal Planet," October 27, 2009, http://www.wfmz.com/news/Local-Woman-On-Animal-Planet/-/121458/348544/-/wewobb/-/index.html.

14 Barela, "The Scorpion Queen."

15 Ibid.

16 Kathryn McMackin, "Seven-Year-Old Cochranite Viciously Attacked by Pit Bull," *Cochrane Eagle*, January 16, 2013, http://www.cochraneeagle.com/article/20130116/COE0801/301169970/-1/coe/seven-year-old-cochranite-viciously-attacked-by-pit-bull.

18 "Chimpanzee Owner: 'Send Police with a Gun,'" *Sky News*, February 18, 2009, http://news.sky.com/story/670383/chimpanzee-owner-send-police-with-a-gun.

19 "Animal Experts Baffled by Chimp Attack," *USA Today*, February 18, 2009, http://usatoday30.usatoday.com/news/nation/2009-02-18-chimpanzee-attack_N.htm?csp=usat.me.

20 "Chimp Attack Victim Charla Nash Shows Her Face," *Oprah.com*, November 11, 2009, http://www.oprah.com/oprahshow/Chimp-Attack-Victim-Charla-Nash-Shows-Her-Face.

20 Katie Moisse, "Charla Nash Gets Face Transplant after Chimp Attack," *ABC News*, June 10, 2011, http://abcnews.go.com/Health/Wellness/charla-nash-receives-full-face-transplant-chimp-attack/story?id=13810279#.Ucm1JD54Znc.

20 "Chimp Attack Victim Charla Nash Shows Her Face."

20 Linda Carroll, "Chimp Attack Victim Speaks about New Face, New Hopes," *Today*, November 21, 2011, http://www.today.com/id/45380267/ns/today-today_health/t/chimp-attack-victim-speaks-about-new-face-new-hopes.

22 Kia Hall Hayes, "Slidell Boy Recounts Fight with 'Godzilla' Gator," *nola.com*, August 22, 2008, http://www.nola.com/news/index.ssf/2008/08/gator_boy_photo_video_for_coll.html.

23 Ibid.

24 Mike Celizic, "Dolphins Save Surfer from Becoming Shark's Bait," *Today*, November 8, 2007, http://www.today.com/id/21689083/ns/today-today_news/t/dolphins-save-surfer-becoming-sharks-bait.

25 Todd Endris, "A Circle of Dolphins," *Angels on Earth*, July/August 2009, 32–36.

26 Ibid.

27 Ibid.

INDEX

PHOTO ACKNOWLEDGMENTS

The images in this book are used with the permission of: © Biosphoto/SuperStock, pp. 4, 5, 15; © eXpose/Shutterstock Images, p. 6; © Milo Burcham/Alaska Stock - Design Pics/SuperStock, p. 7; © outdoorsman/Shutterstock Images, p. 8; © Corbis/SuperStock, p. 9; © Lido Vizzutti/Flathead Beacon/AP Images, p. 10; © Niki Desautels/Seattle Post-Intelligencer/AP Images, p. 11; © Staff Sgt. Michael R. Holzworth/US Air Force, p. 12; © Imagemore/SuperStock, p. 13; © Marko Drobnjakovic/AP Images, p. 14; © Exactostock/SuperStock, p. 16; © Torin Halsey/Wichita Falls Times Record News/AP Images, p. 17; © James Crisp/AP Images, p. 18; © Paul Desmarais/The Stamford Advocate/AP Images, p. 19; © Lightchaser Photography/Brigham and Women's Hospital/AP Images, p. 20; © Jessica Hill/AP Images, p. 21; © Bonnie Fink/Shutterstock Images, p. 22; © Sorbis/Shutterstock Images, p. 23; © Jamen Percy/Shutterstock Images, p. 24; © Cliff Russell/Solent News/Rex Features/AP Images, p. 25; © Jim Tucker/AP Images, p. 26; © Epic Stock Media/Shutterstock Images, p. 27; © Sergey Uryadnikov/Shutterstock Images, p. 28; © Alta Oosthuizen/Shutterstock Images, p. 29 (top); © smuay/Shutterstock Images, p. 29 (bottom).

Front Cover: © Seread/Dreamstime.com.